BRAD PITT

CRAZYSEXYCOOL

ELISABETH SHUE

CRAZYSEXYCOOL

EDITOR HOLLY GEORGE-WARREN
ASSOCIATE EDITOR SHAWN DAHL
EDITORIAL ASSISTANT GREG EMMANUEL
EDITORIAL CONTRIBUTOR DAVID WILD

DESIGNER FRED WOODWARD
PHOTO EDITOR JENNIFER CRANDALL
DESIGN ASSOCIATE AMY GOLDFARB

COVER

DREW BARRYMORE	MARK SELIGER
LIV TYLER	MARK SELIGER
LENNY KRAVITZ	RUVEN AFANADOR
CINDY CRAWFORD	DAVIS FACTOR
SAMUEL L. JACKSON	MELODIE McDANIEL
ASHLEY JUDD	MARK SELIGER
AIDAN QUINN	DAVID BAILEY
TOM HANKS	MARK SELIGER
JODIE FOSTER	MARK SELIGER
JAKOB DYLAN	LEN IRISH
LISA LOEB	KEVIN WESTENBERG
HENRY ROLLINS	PEGGY SIROTA
GILLIAN ANDERSON	ANDREW SOUTHAM
GWYNETH PALTROW	STEVEN SEBRING
JERRY SEINFELD	FRANK OCKENFELS 3
HELEN HUNT	MARK SELIGER
GARY OLDMAN	PEGGY SIROTA
EMMA THOMPSON	NEIL DAVENPORT
TIMOTHY HUTTON	JOHN HUBA
CHRISTIAN SLATER	MARK SELIGER
GEENA DAVIS	LANCE STAEDLER
MATT DILLON	LANCE STAEDLER
PATRICIA ARQUETTE	BUTCH BELAIR
COOLIO	ALBERT WATSON
KENNEDY	MARK SELIGER
VANESSA WILLIAMS	NAOMI KALTMAN
CHRIS ISAAK	MICHAEL MILLER
JULIA LOUIS-DREYFUS	JON RAGEL
JASON PRIESTLEY	LANCE STAEDLER
MIRA SORVINO	GUZMAN
CONAN O'BRIEN	LEN IRISH
ANTONIO BANDERAS	LANCE STAEDLER
WHOOPI GOLDBERG	MARK SELIGER
DAVID DUCHOVNY	JON RAGEL
CHRISSIE HYNDE	MARK SELIGER
DAVID SCHWIMMER	MARK SELIGER
ANGELA BASSETT	DAVIS FACTOR

First Edition

ISBN 0-316-55353-0

Library of Congress
Catalog Card Number
96-77341

10 9 8 7 6 5 4 3 2 1

IM

Published simultaneously
in Canada by Little,
Brown & Company
(Canada) Limited

Printed in Singapore

ACKNOWLEDGMENTS

Barbara O'Dair, Richard Baker, Jann S. Wenner, Kent Brownridge, John Lagana, Daniel Stark,
Rachel Knepfer, Geraldine Hessler, Eric Siry, Pamela Berry, Willis Caster, Tom Worley, Vicki Puorro,
Rossana Shokrian, Jennifer Wesley, Kristin Dymitruk, Sara Kalish, Michael Pietsch, Clif Gaskill,
Bryan Quible, Sarah Lazin, Tracie Matthews, Susan Richardson, Will Rigby, Nawal Asfour, Howard
Musk, Nora Krug, Marianne Burke, Steve Warner, Miriam Abdessemed, Kimberly Feldman,
Juliette Knight, Cathy Weiner, Sofi Dillof, Art + Commerce, CPI, Michael Ginsburg and Associates,
Outline Press Syndicate, the Botaish Group, Lynn LaMoine, Visages and all the photographers
whose work appears here. Also thanks to the subjects and their support staff.

LITTLE, BROWN AND COMPANY

BOSTON   NEW YORK   TORONTO   LONDON

CRAZYSEXYCOOL

BY THE EDITORS OF US MAGAZINE

ODE TO A '90s BABE

by david wild

{ and other visions of nowness }

{

When old age shall this generation waste Thou shalt remain, in midst of other woe Than ours, a friend to man, to whom thou say'st "Beauty is truth, truth beauty," that is all Ye know on earth, and all ye need to know

}

T

HE PRECEDING ANTICOMMERCIAL MESSAGE comes to you directly from John Keats' "Ode to a Grecian Urn," written way back in 1819, a romantic, carefree era long before the fall of Communism and the rise of Courtney Love. At the risk of having my poetic license revoked, I would like to think if the old Keatster were still around putting quill to Powerbook he might forget about urns entirely and instead be penning "Ode to Mark Seliger's Portrait of Drew Barrymore." After all, the pretty truth of the matter is that Seliger's stunning photo and the numerous other startling images gracing this lovely book you're holding in your hands are truly things of Nineties beauty. ■■ To each and every one of the crazy, sexy and cool kids featured in these visually arresting pages, I can only echo the immortal words spoken by the late, great philosopher king of cool Sammy Davis Jr. to singer Belinda Carlisle when he spotted her in a Los Angeles restaurant back in those golden go-go Eighties. "You are a vision of nowness," the Candy Man told her in pure Sammy-speak. ■■ Once upon a time, even before those Rat-Packing days of wine and

Sammy, Whistler's Mother may well have represented our notion of amazing grace. But in today's youth-oriented – okay, youth-*obsessed* – culture, most of us probably would be far more interested in checking out an arty portrait of Whistler's daughter or son, particularly if she or he were famous, artistically inclined and – this *never* hurts – scantily clad.

All of this gloriously high-brow rambling brings to mind that glorious conversation of yore when the always wordy F. Scott Fitzgerald tried to convince a typically tipsy Ernest Hemingway of his belief that "the rich, young and famous are different from you and me." Hemingway – being Hemingway – responded, "You're right, they have more money and look *much* better when posed in *US* magazine."

Ladies and gents, the sordid truth of the matter is that the people in this book *are* different from you and me. And while one hesitates to make any value judgments whatsoever in this age of political correctness, the visions of nowness collected in this book clearly define resonant contemporary archetypes for what we, as a society of voyeuristic stargazers, now consider most beautiful, audacious and appealing. In other words, they are *Crazy Sexy Cool*.

And we're *not*.

KAY, IN OUR DEFENSE, WE'RE NOT exactly sex-appeal–challenged either. Occasionally we're pretty damn cute ourselves, even without the aid of all those hair and makeup spin doctors who help the stars shine so brightly in *US*. Still, the undeniable fact remains that the pop cultural figures photographed so monumentally herein are bigger – and arguably a little better – than life. They are, in a variety of ways, iconic, and even if they weren't, the extraordinarily talented photographers whose work appears in *US* and in this book would have somehow found a means to make them appear to be anyway.

What exactly – you hypothetically ask – does it mean to be *Crazy Sexy Cool* today? In coining the phrase, the three lovely women in TLC captured exactly today's version of those qualities that have long been the very soul of that wacky little cool-kids club that we call pop culture. And despite what any pretentious agenda-toting blowhards like myself might have you believe, the truth is that Elvis Presley did not become the King of Rock & Roll just because he bravely merged some black and white music idioms. No, the fact is that the King hit it big in part because he was a wild hunka, hunka burning love who turned on a significant part of the planet by swiveling his hips and sneering regally.

By the same token, James Dean was not simply a great thespian and a resonant symbol for disenfranchised youth of the Fifties – he was also a pouty-looking giant stud, just like Luke Perry. Marilyn Monroe was not initially a culturally significant screen goddess. Like Madonna after her, she first caught our eye as a sexy pop tart of the very first order. Even the Beatles did not start off as spokesmen for a generation – first they were four fabulously cute guys with great haircuts who wanted to rather indiscriminately hold our hands.

Making a real impact in our youth culture has long been – at least in part – about getting the opposite sex to want to sleep with you and the same sex to want to look like you – usually with enough room left over for a generous serving of gender-bending crossover. And while modern celebrity is by no means strictly a mere beauty contest, the reality remains that looks and image *do* count. Ladies and germs, there's a very good reason that they call it show business – what you have to show the world matters. And as the pages of *Crazy Sexy Cool* vividly demonstrate, it turns out that many of the beautiful people are – hold those presses! – *beautiful*.

Same as it ever was.

You could argue that any culture that worships and rewards the young and beautiful – whom the gods have already rewarded

anyway, the lucky little photogenic bastards and bitches – instead of, say, schoolteachers is shallow and wildly misguided. But to hell with substance, we are for better and for worse living in a time when the business of America *is* show business. Celebrity in all its varied and sometimes scary permutations is what turns us on today, serving as our benign sort of new improved, socially acceptable pornography. These professional entertainers not only create the movies, TV shows and albums that we enjoy: They also serve as our celebrated flesh for fantasy.

Some of the young performers featured here are tremendously talented individuals on the cutting edge in their fields of artistic endeavor and who would be well known no matter what they looked like. Others arguably couldn't act or sing or play their way out of a small, preripped paper bag. Finally, though, as Bill Murray tells the troops in the epic *Meatballs*, it *just* doesn't matter. To abusively paraphrase some wise words the late Lord Acton once said about power, fame tends to charm and absolute fame charms absolutely.

In our undying desire of the freshly iconic, we late–Twentieth Century humans are utterly and perhaps unhealthily insatiable. Once upon a time we hungered for a new Elvis, a new Brando, a new Dylan. These days, we cry out regularly for the next Kurt Cobain and a newly rising River Phoenix. Now more than ever, the savage beast that is our popular culture demands to be fed constantly; thus a magazine like *US* is there to provide a tasty snack for both the eyes and the mind.

EST THERE BE ANY confusion, the photos at the heart of this book are not just snapshots of today's leading pieces of ass. These are provocative pieces of art that capture the attitude-drenched, in-your-face spirit of the folks who strike our collective fancy as being *Crazy Sexy Cool* in the 1990s. These color and black & white images – playful and insightful, haunting and hilarious – are the extraordinary work of many of the most distinctive and influential photographers working in the Nineties, including Mark Seliger, Peggy Sirota, Mary Ellen Mark, Lance Staedler, Davis Factor, Brigitte Lacombe, Anton Corbijn, Steven Meisel, Frank Ockenfels 3, Jon Ragel, Dewey Nicks, Guzman, Butch Belair, Stephen Danelian, Matthew Rolston, Len Irish, Greg Gorman, Naomi Kaltman and Max Vadukul.

US magazine editor-in-chief Jann S. Wenner's strong and enduring commitment to presenting great photography is by now well established. At *Rolling Stone* in the Seventies and early Eighties, Wenner gave Annie Leibovitz and many other photographers a remarkable platform to largely define popular portraiture in much the way *Life* had in an earlier era. Now, in the Nineties, he has given Mark Seliger and the photographers whose work appears in *US* the artistic leeway to present many of the decade's most compelling and ultimately telling images.

I THINK WHAT WE'RE REALLY TRYING TO SHOW is the intimate side of some very public people," says Seliger in a rare moment between shoots. "The truth is people become more interesting when they agree to let their guard down and let us unveil them a bit. Take the process as far as we possibly can, make an event of it." And how exactly is that achieved at *US?* "There are two ways," Seliger explains. "You can either try to show the person behind the persona or you can play off that persona and try to do something totally different with it. We're in a time in portraiture when anything goes."

Of course living in an anything goes era of media overload and rampant celebrity overexposure makes *US*'s mission to be a youthful, energetic, vivid and insightful entertainment magazine all the more challenging.

"That's our mandate," says *US* editor Barbara O'Dair. "We strive to get beyond the rehash of career and chronology to give our reader some real insight into these celebrated people." For O'Dair, the same rules apply to the magazine's portraits as its profiles. "We want to give our subjects texture and presence," she says. "We're looking to be surprised by images, the kind that jump out and grab us by the throat – or stick their tongues down your throat. Ultimately those are the sort of photographs that make the magazine a living, breathing thing."

That sort of ambition is infectious.

"We're looking to create truly monumental images," adds *US* art director Richard Baker. "It's like those great Hollywood magazines our parents read or *Life* and *Look* – you'd look at the photos and think, How the hell did they get this person to *do* that?"

ROM PERSONAL EXPERIENCE, I can report that having a photographer like Seliger working on a story that you're writing means discovering you have a dream collaborator, an ingenious partner in crime who's going to surprise you every time by telling the story in a way you never could. Forget all that clichéd crap about a picture being worth only a thousand words: Based on some of my collaborations with Mark and some of his camera-toting brothers and sisters whose work appears here, I can state unequivocally that in our new math some photographs are worth *at least* five thousand words.

There's certainly no shortage of stripped-down stars gracing the pages of *Crazy Sexy Cool*, and that's only right since we're living in a time when artfulness and trashiness commingle freely. Yet as Tom Wolfe once wrote about an "exposed" subject depicted on the cover of *Rolling Stone*, "The nudity was the least of it. The startling part was the sense of vulnerability and self-revelation."

There always seems to be some level of two-way seduction involved in the photographic process. Indeed, I have long noticed that there is *something* about Mark Seliger in particular that seems to make famous people want to disrobe. I've always thought this must be an ideal quality to have when you're dating. And while I'm very fond of the guy, personally speaking I've never even taken off my jacket in front of him. Perhaps that's what has held me back from true stardom.

Enough inter-office praise, the book's the thing. Some of you photophiles may recall a pair of important works of photojournalism published earlier in this century: *Let Us Now Praise Famous Men* with photos by Walker Evans and text by James Agee and *You Have Seen Their Faces* by Margaret Bourke-White with text by Erskine Caldwell. And as we stare down our nation's next not-so-great depression, you might want to think of *Crazy Sexy Cool* as *Let Us Now Praise Famous People* or alternately *You Have Seen Their Faces and Possibly Some Other Body Parts Too*. In his preamble to *Let Us Now Praise Famous Men*, James Agee wrote, "If I could do it, I'd do no writing at all here. It would be photographs; the rest would be fragments of cloth, bits of cotton, lumps of earth, records of speech, pieces of wood and iron, phials of odors, plates of food and excrement...."

Well, fortunately for you the reader, there are not too many more words left to read in *Crazy Sexy Cool*, and no odors either as far as we're aware. Instead, what you get are photos that capture the essence of our times by focusing on the individuals who we, as a society of pop-culture-obsessed voyeurs, talk about, think about, argue about and even dream about.

How exactly have these celebrated individuals won our hearts? Let us count the ways.

HE TRUTH IS WE LIVE IN VERY BLURRY times within the creative arts. Actors like Johnny Depp and Keanu Reeves do double duty as moonlighting rock stars. Rock stars like Chris Isaak want to act or attempt to be an alterna-film mogul like Michael Stipe. Video vixens like Alicia Silverstone turn into box-office divas. A model, Cindy Crawford, dares to act and is paid to do so. The rest of us sit back, enjoy the show and think about sleeping with them – though, unfortunately, being celebrities, they generally choose to inbreed.

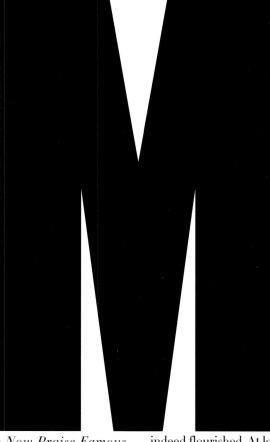

OST OF THE SUBJECTS seen in *Crazy Sexy Cool* are celebrated young'uns – fin de siècle stars too young to have joined the Brat Pack, not to mention the Rat Pack. A few youth-deprived subjects like Dennis Hopper and Jack Nicholson appear here because they remain ageless by virtue of their ongoing and enduring coolness. As we've already seen too many times in recent years, fame has a way of eating its young. Fortunately, the groovy lads and lassies featured in *Crazy Sexy Cool* have survived, indeed flourished. At least in these photos they will stay forever young and, at the very least, momentarily hip. Having personally interviewed many of these folks, I'd like to tell you that each and every one of them is the salt of the earth, a down-to-earth boy/girl-next-door type who you'd totally love if only you met him or her. As I said, I'd *like* to tell you that, but I'm not getting paid enough to perpetuate any lies that big. The boring truth, however, is that none of them ever revealed themselves to me to be anything less than charming.

And, finally, the true power of *Crazy Sexy Cool* is that the photographers – the artistically investigative photojournalists, if you will – have turned a rather neat trick here. In collaborating with their beloved subjects, they have managed to show us something both new and familiar about the popular, sometimes overexposed figures of our time. And in fine postmodern form, these images both celebrate the starmaking machinery and shed a new, flattering but revealing light on the whole *mishegoss*. These photos, at their best, are visual revelations, both of the manner in which we perceive these young lions and lionesses and of who they really, truly are. We live in a time when seeing is way beyond believing. Our cameras rarely lie, and when the camera does lie, it sure as hell lies *beautifully*. Even in the transitory pop culture of these *Crazy Sexy Cool* times, John Keats was right: "A thing of beauty is a joy forever."

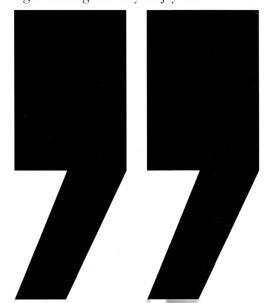

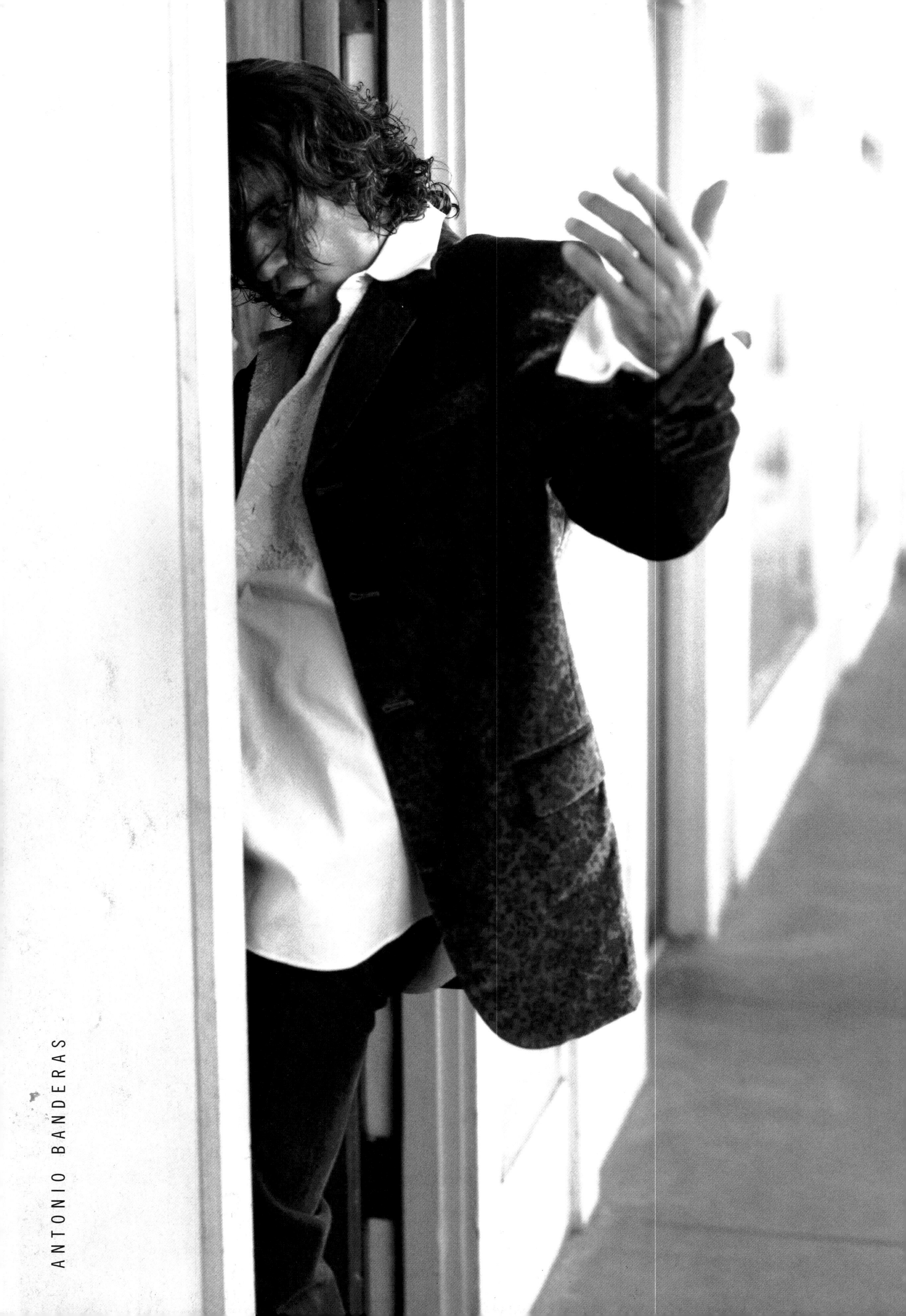

ANTONIO BANDERAS

KENNETH BRANAGH

PATRICIA ARQUETTE

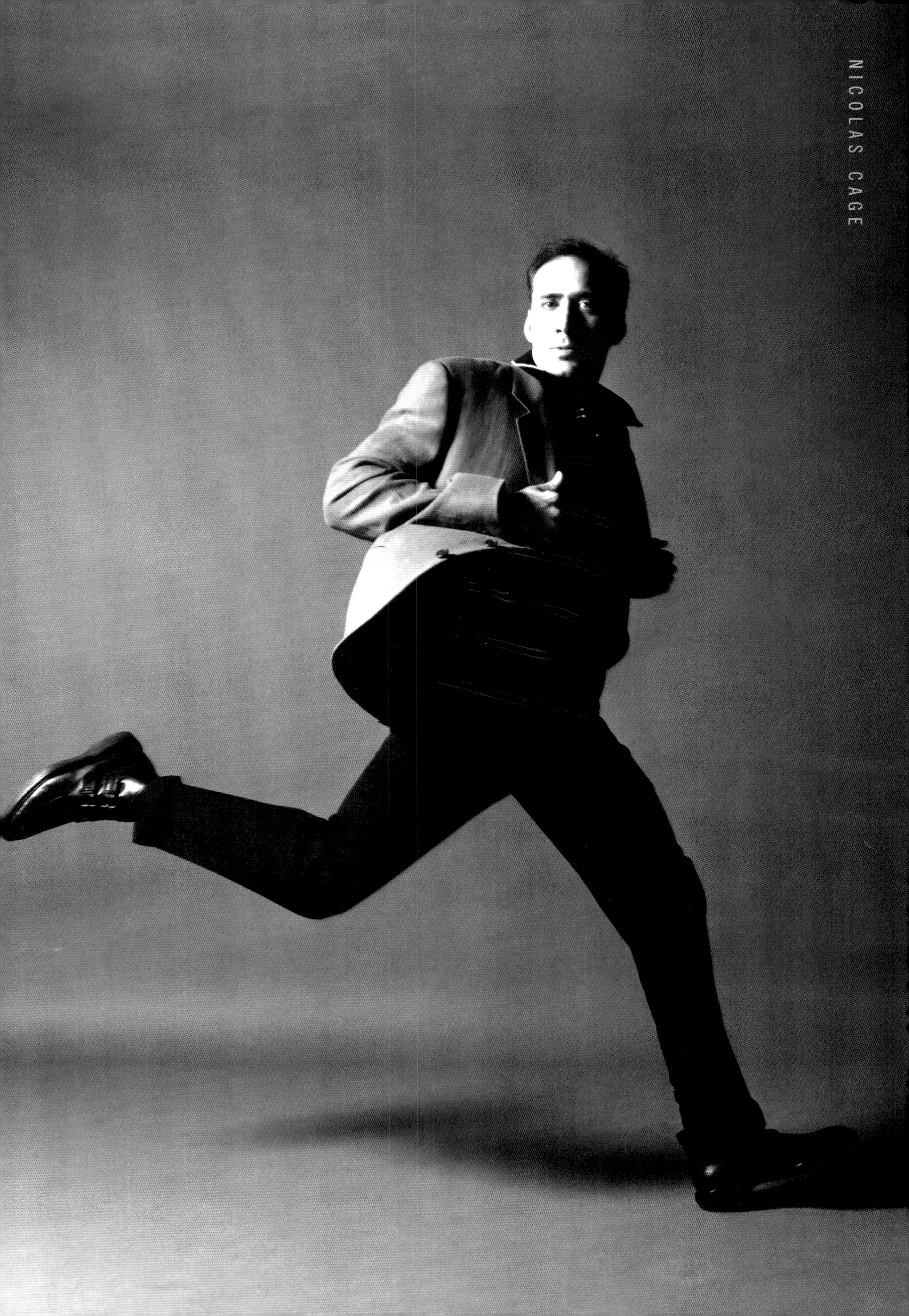

NICOLAS CAGE

KIM BASINGER & ALEC BALDWIN

KATO KAELIN.

I THINK IN my singing I allow myself the luxury of vulnerability, which I don't really allow in my personal life. I think I'm just...very masked, I've got a poker face. But in singing you can't help exposing your vulnerability.

FOR A LONG TIME I FELT like an anarchist, wanting to destroy everything which seemed in the way. But that's a hard label to live up to. I don't want to be wild every day.

I BELIEVE IN the Wild Man. It's that instinctual, innate part of you, your power, that if used constructively can be an incredibly productive force. But off-kilter the least bit, it'll kill you. I'm real intrigued by that edge. It can create an unpredictable, dangerous performance. I want the Wild Man in my work.

SEAN PENN

I HONESTLY DON'T give a fuck what anybody thinks about me – except the people close to me.

MY CHARACTERS ARE slightly damaged, slightly neurotic, but with an incredible determination and an undying spirit. No matter how battered and bruised they might become, they have this will to persevere.

I PLAY DISENFRANCHISED people that are in most cases pushed out of the way or cast aside. Part of my agenda with that is out of some kind of need to save them. To be representative of those people.

EVERYBODY PUTS a label on it and calls me a bad boy or a delinquent or a rebel or one of those horrible terms. But to me, it was much more *curiosity*.

DREW BARRYMORE

I GET TO BE A KID NOW, because I wasn't a kid when I was supposed to be one. But in some ways, I'm an old woman – lived it, seen it, done it, been there, have the T-shirt.

OK, I'M 37. I'm not supposed to do certain things – speak up for myself, change my life. I'm too old. Well, FUCK THAT!

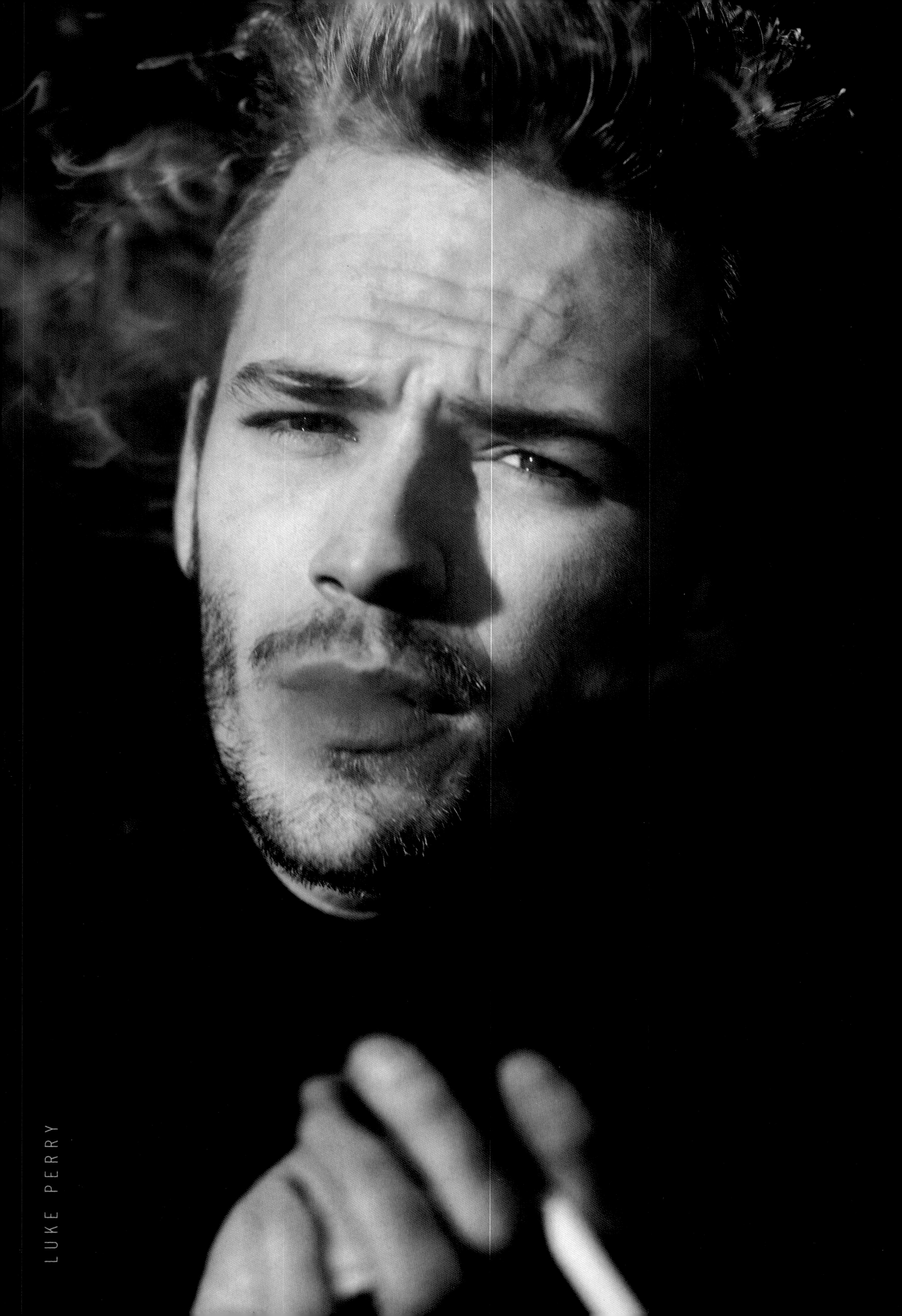

LUKE PERRY

WHOOPI GOLDBERG

LEA THOMPSON

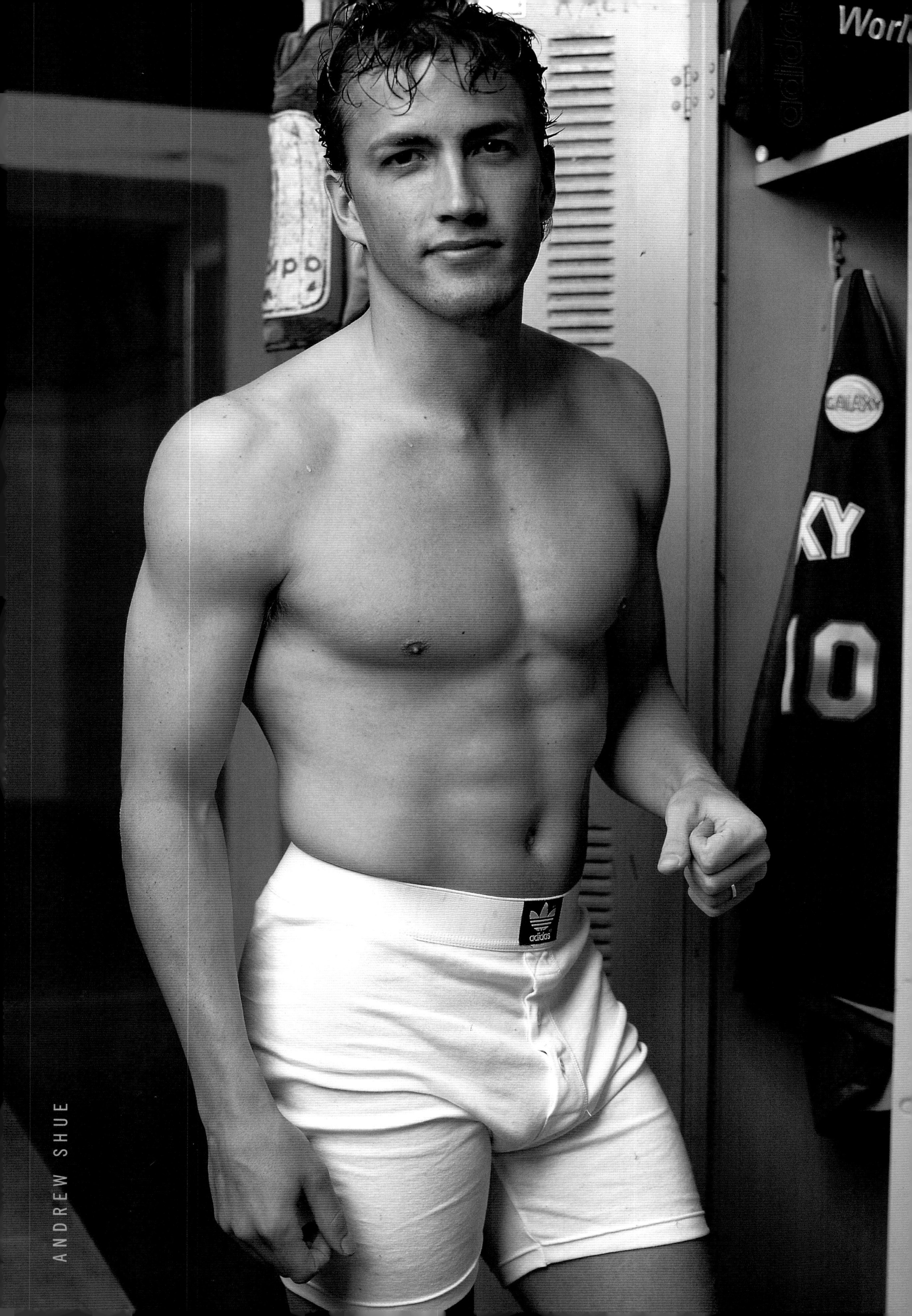

ANDREW SHUE

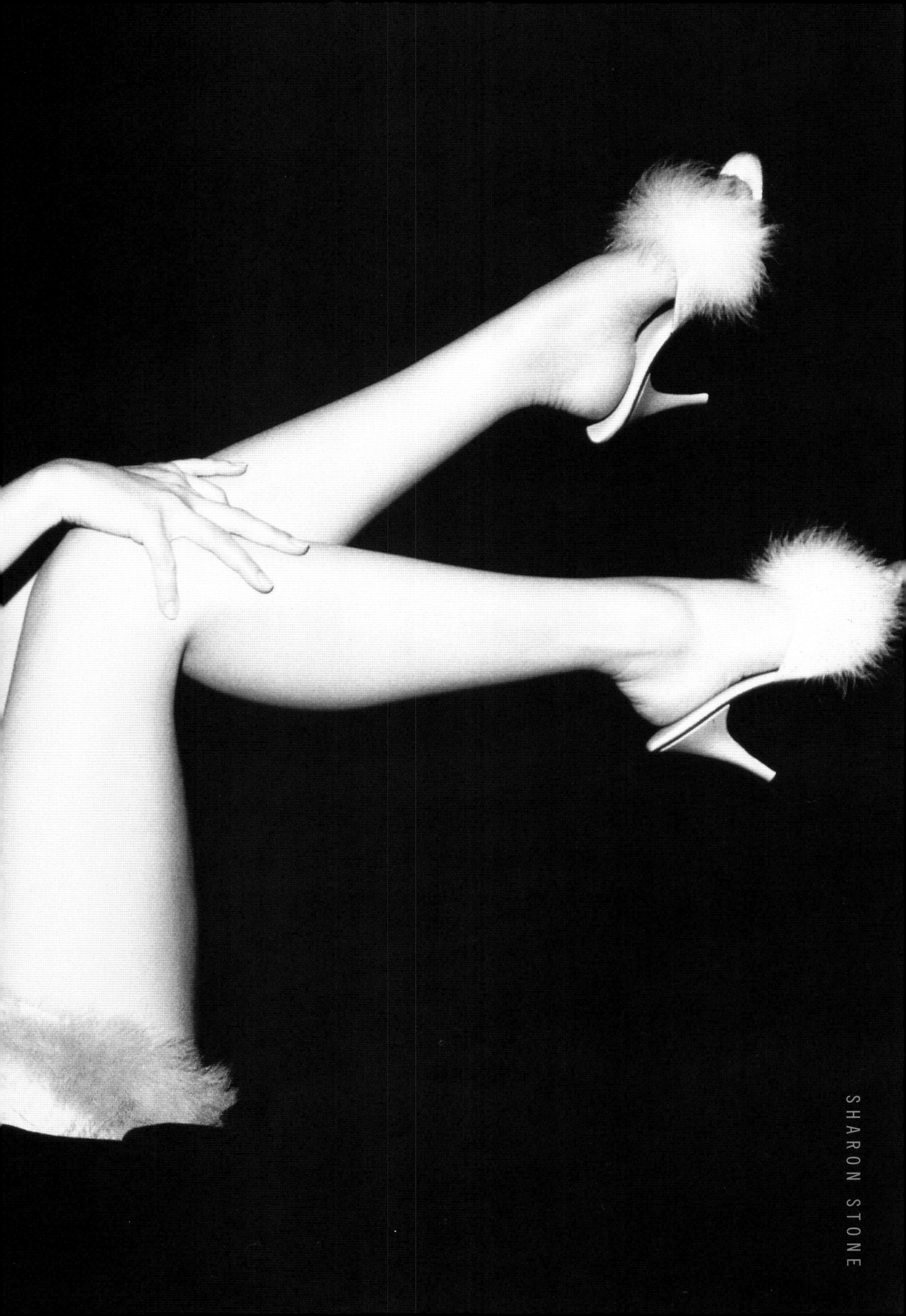

SHARON STONE

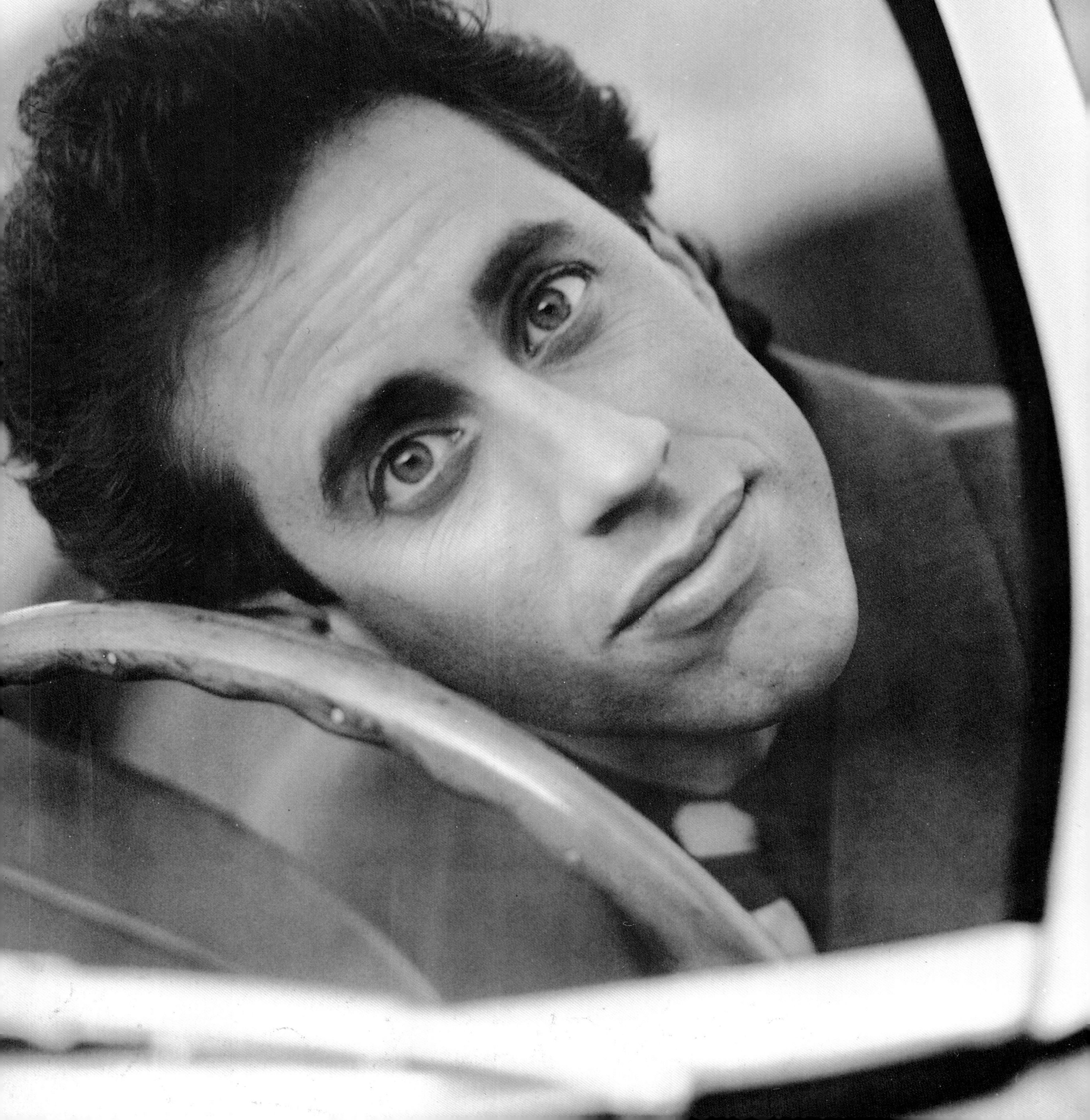

MELISSA ETHERIDGE

SOMEONE ONCE SAID that actors are all a bunch of sissies dressed up in frocks. That's not far from the truth.

THE PEOPLE WHO own studios didn't get to where they were by being dumb business-men. They aren't going to pay me one penny more than I'm worth, especially in this marketplace. They wouldn't pay it if I wasn't worth it. And the day I'm not, they won't.

THE AMOUNT of money that I'm getting is so ridiculous that it's basically like looking at a Monopoly board.

COME FROM THE heartland, and that's the kind of music I make. I'm not a trend.

I MADE THIS MOVIE *Super Mario Bros.*, and my son said, "Dad, why'd you make that?" I said, "So I can afford to buy you shoes." He said, "Dad, I don't need shoes that badly."

I'M A MOVIE STAR. I am! You know what a movie star is? He's the guy like me who gets paid to do these movies and go all around the world and go to these big, honking fetes. But I think I have been able to bend it so it is on my terms at the same time. I don't have bodyguards. My assistant is my entourage. Show business with a human face, I call it.

TOM HANKS

IT'S VERY EMOTIONAL to have worked this long and to have had so many moments of real doubt and then finally realize that it's possible to do good work.

I'VE BEEN AFRAID of being typecast, afraid I'd have to hear "Yabba Dabba Doo" for the rest of my life. But it's better than shoveling dirt for a living.

DENNIS HOPPER

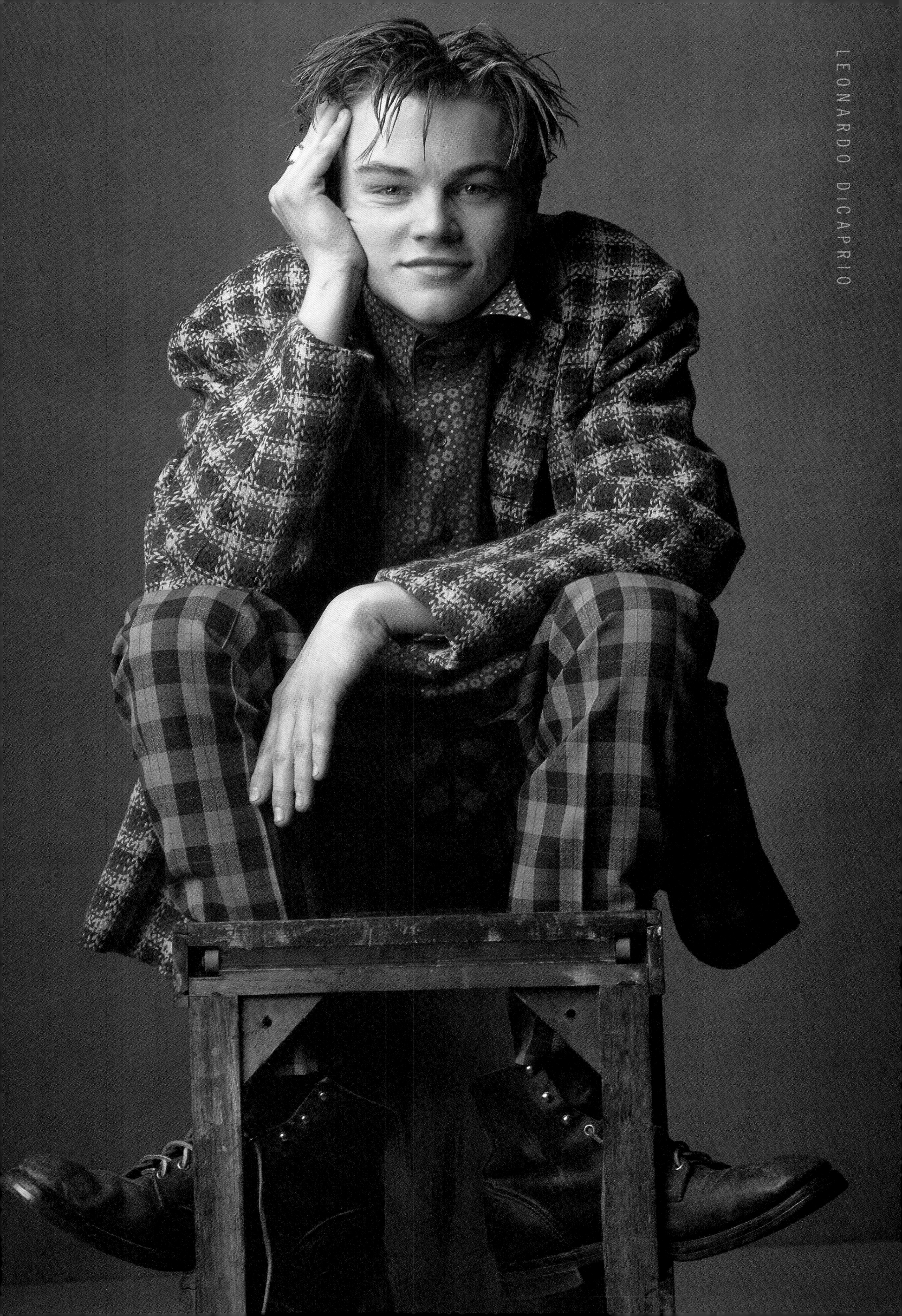

LEONARDO DICAPRIO

PATRICIA ARQUETTE

WHEN I USED TO go to gas pumps, I'd pretend that was my penis. After I'd pump gas, I'd shake it. I love the idea of having a penis for a little bit, just to understand the other side.

EMMA THOMPSON

MARRIAGE is an extremely dangerous step—so don't do it until you've shagged everything with a pulse.

JERRY SEINFELD

EVERYONE IS looking for good sex, good food and a good laugh.

I REALLY don't know that much about sex. I can be very sexual in my *mind*, of course!

ALICIA SILVERSTONE

IT'S HARD TO DATE actors, but at least they're as troubled and neurotic as you are, so you feel normal.

SARAH JESSICA PARKER

I ALWAYS BROKE UP WITH nonvegetarians. It's like if someone smokes cigarettes and you don't, you don't want to taste that in their mouth.

I WOULDN'T want a penis. It would be like having a third leg. It would seem like a contraption that would get in the way. I think I have a dick in my brain. I don't need to have one between my legs.

IF I SLEPT WITH everyone I was supposed to have, I wouldn't have the energy to eat.

I SUNBATHE on nude beaches. What's the big deal? We're all different sizes. Some of us are just a little bigger than others.

JOHN BARROWMAN

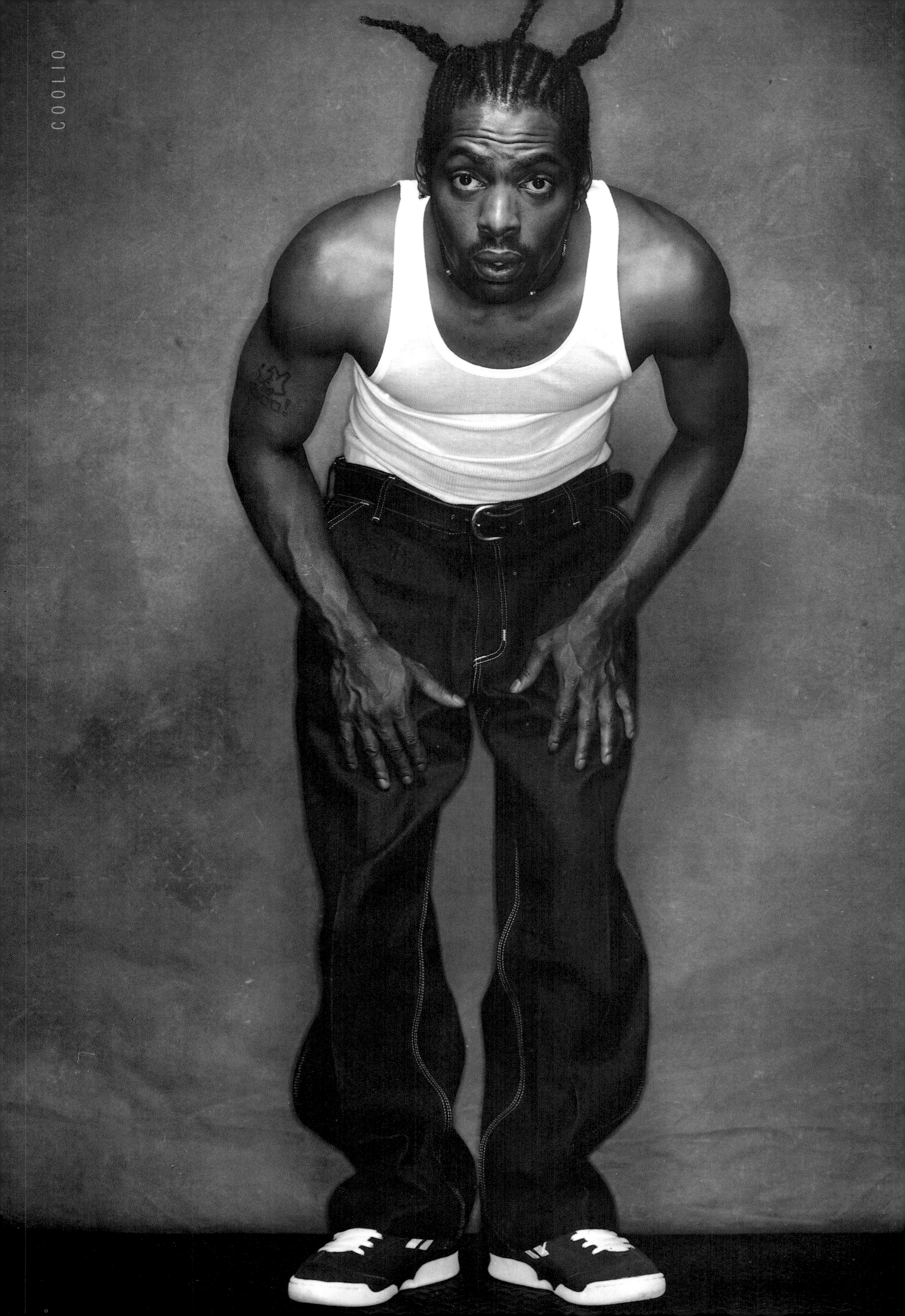

COOLIO

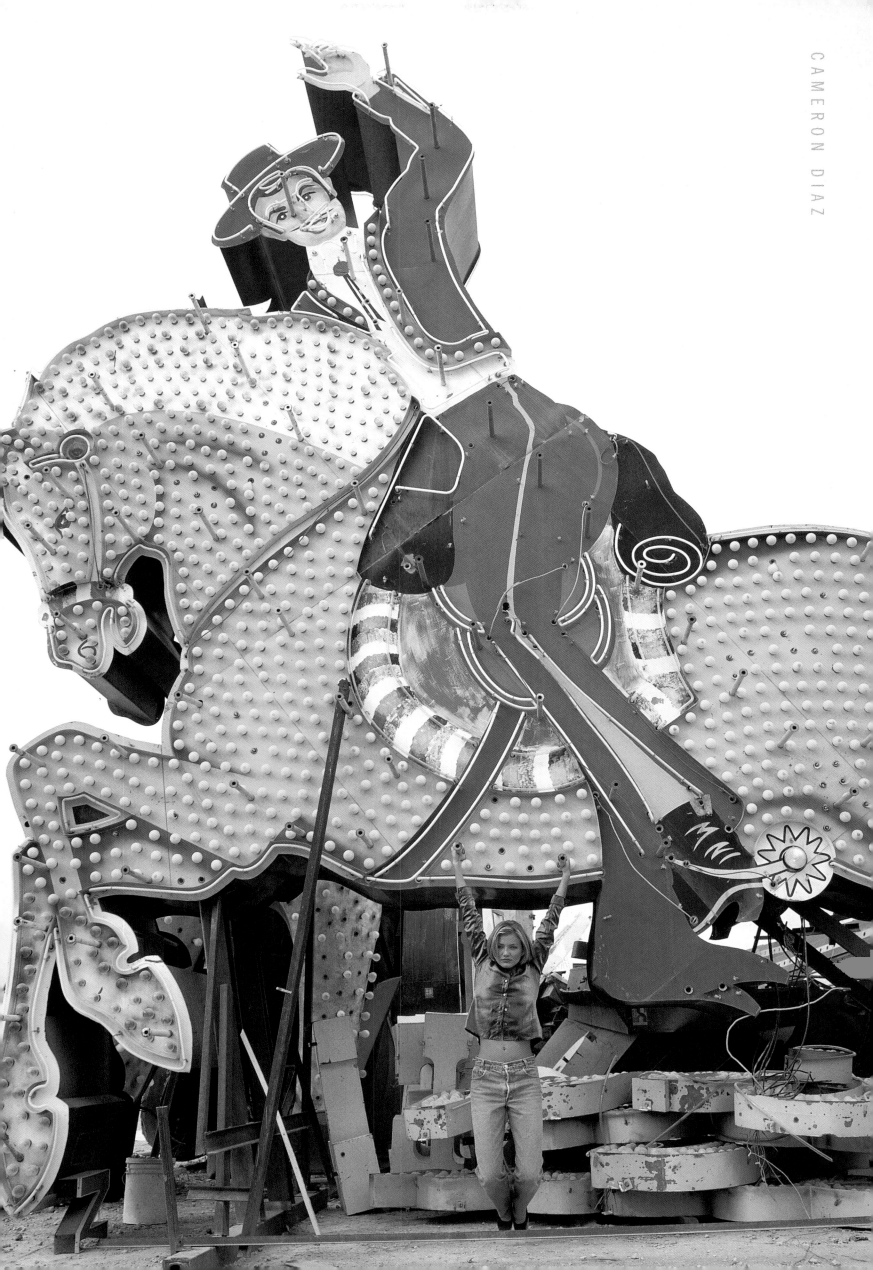

GWYNETH PALTROW

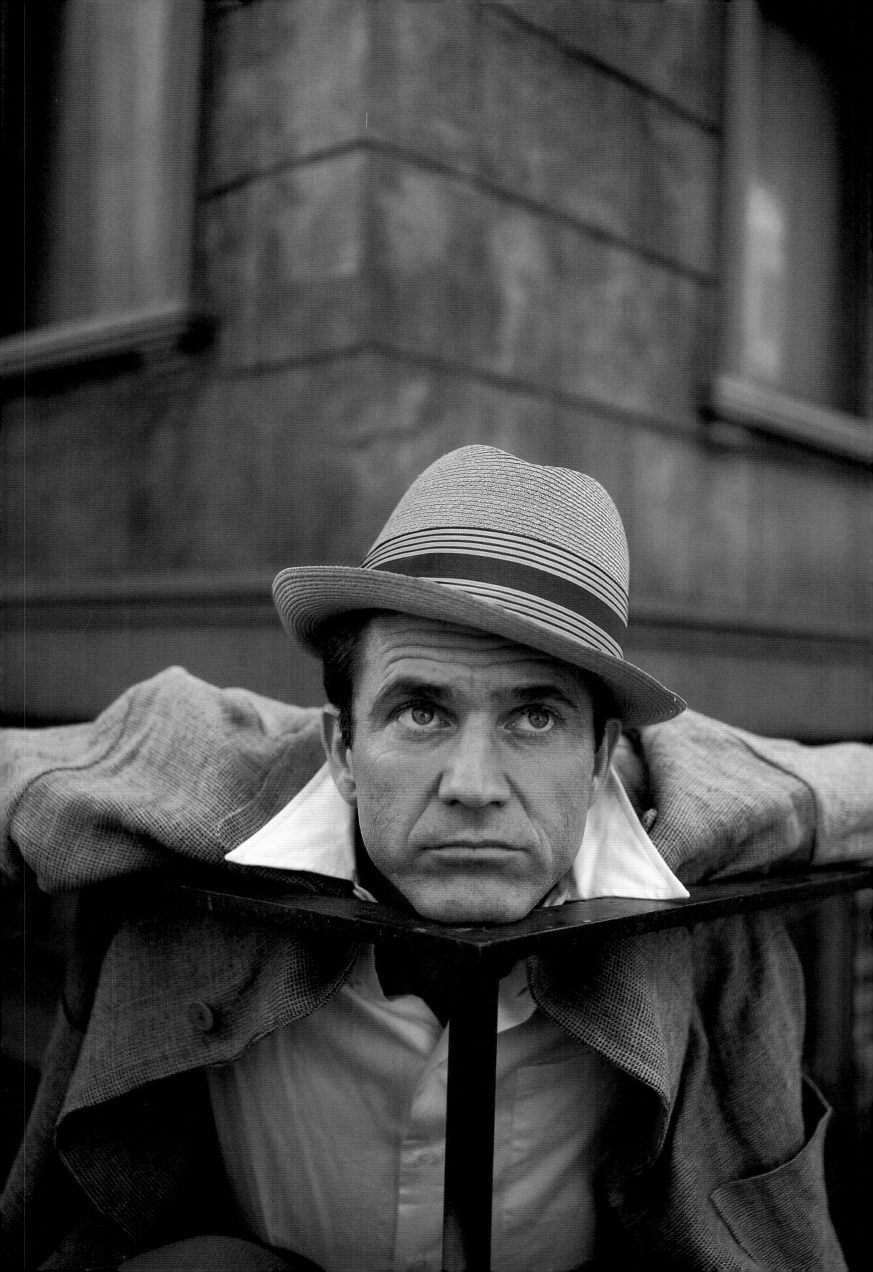

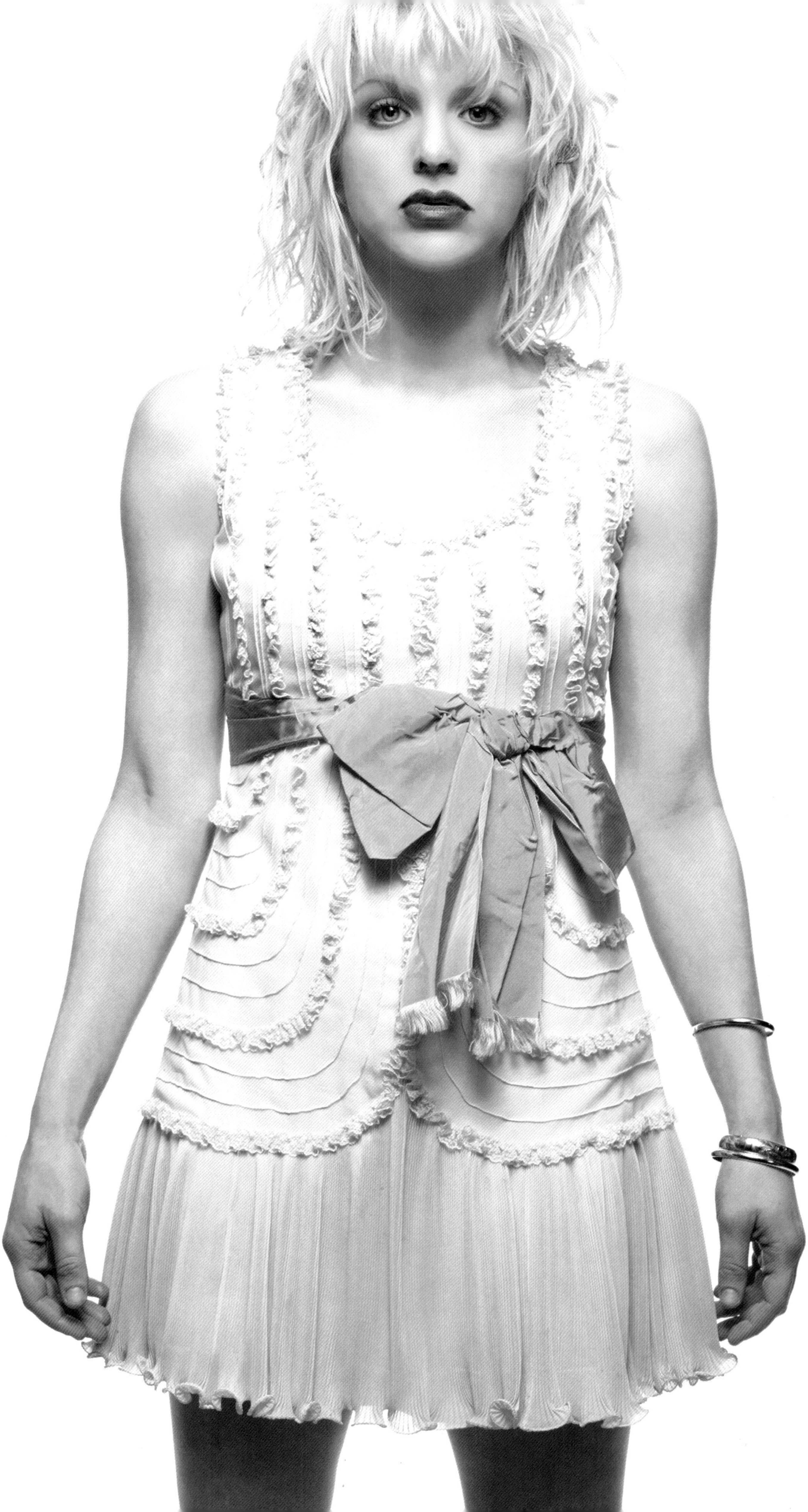

COURTNEY LOVE

JAKOB DYLAN

SOMETIMES what you have in your face doesn't correspond with what you have in your soul.

ANTONIO BANDERAS

WHEN I CAME TO HOLLYWOOD I looked like an inflatable Barbie doll, and nobody wanted me to play anything too edgy. Then it started to become apparent that, you know, I was *good* at that...I never thought that I looked on the outside like I was on the inside. On the inside I feel like a dark Semitic girl with curly hair. I have never felt blond.

OBVIOUSLY, I'm young and crazy and a hormonal psychopath for beautiful women. So why not, in my position, go out with gorgeous girls? If I didn't do that, I don't think I'd be considered normal.

EVERYTHING I WEAR tends to revolve around my breasts. Not because I'm trying to be sexy, but because I just hate wearing a bra!

IN THE MTV ONLINE chat room, I'd write "Kennedy has big, big titties." A lot of times I'd get ignored.

KENNEDY

I DON'T MIND IF SOMEONE THINKS a picture of me decorates their wall nicely. It's weird when you think what people might be doing to it. I just don't want to hear about the graphic details, you know. But if just the way I look can make someone feel good, that's a pretty easy way for me to bring them some pleasure.

CINDY CRAWFORD

I'VE NEVER DONE ANYTHING deliberately sexy. I'm relatively shy about stuff. At the same time it's exciting. But I'm really grateful that I haven't *made* myself on the basis of being sexy. With a lot of actresses, *that's* them. *That's* what they are famous for, *that's* what they've sold themselves as. Maybe I've done a lot of bad movies, but I've never exploited myself.

THE AGE I'M AT NOW, you go from being a young girl to suddenly, really, you blossom into a woman. You ripen, you know? And then you start to rot.

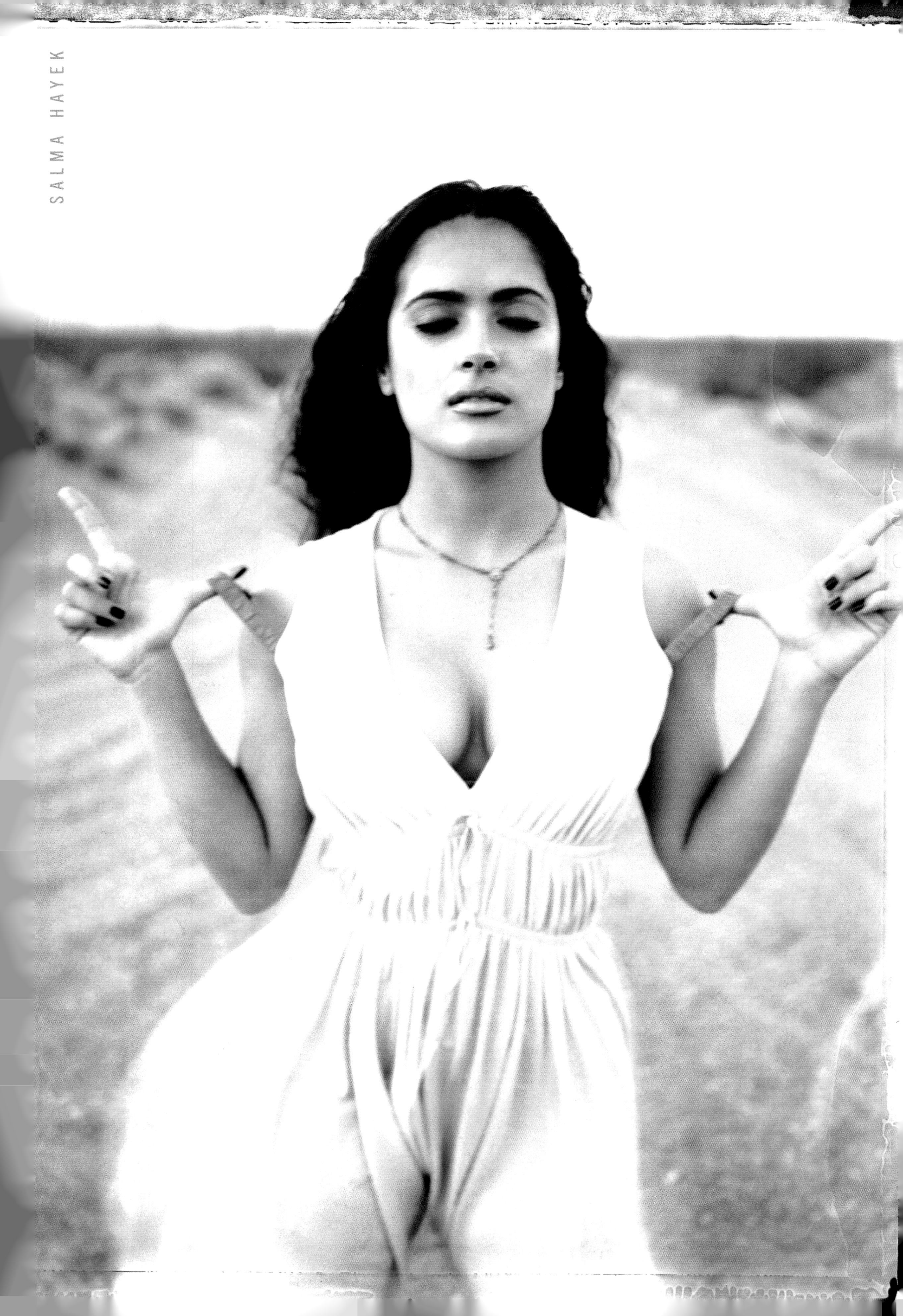

TORI AMOS

BILLY ZANE

ELLEN BARKIN

SARAH JESSICA PARKER

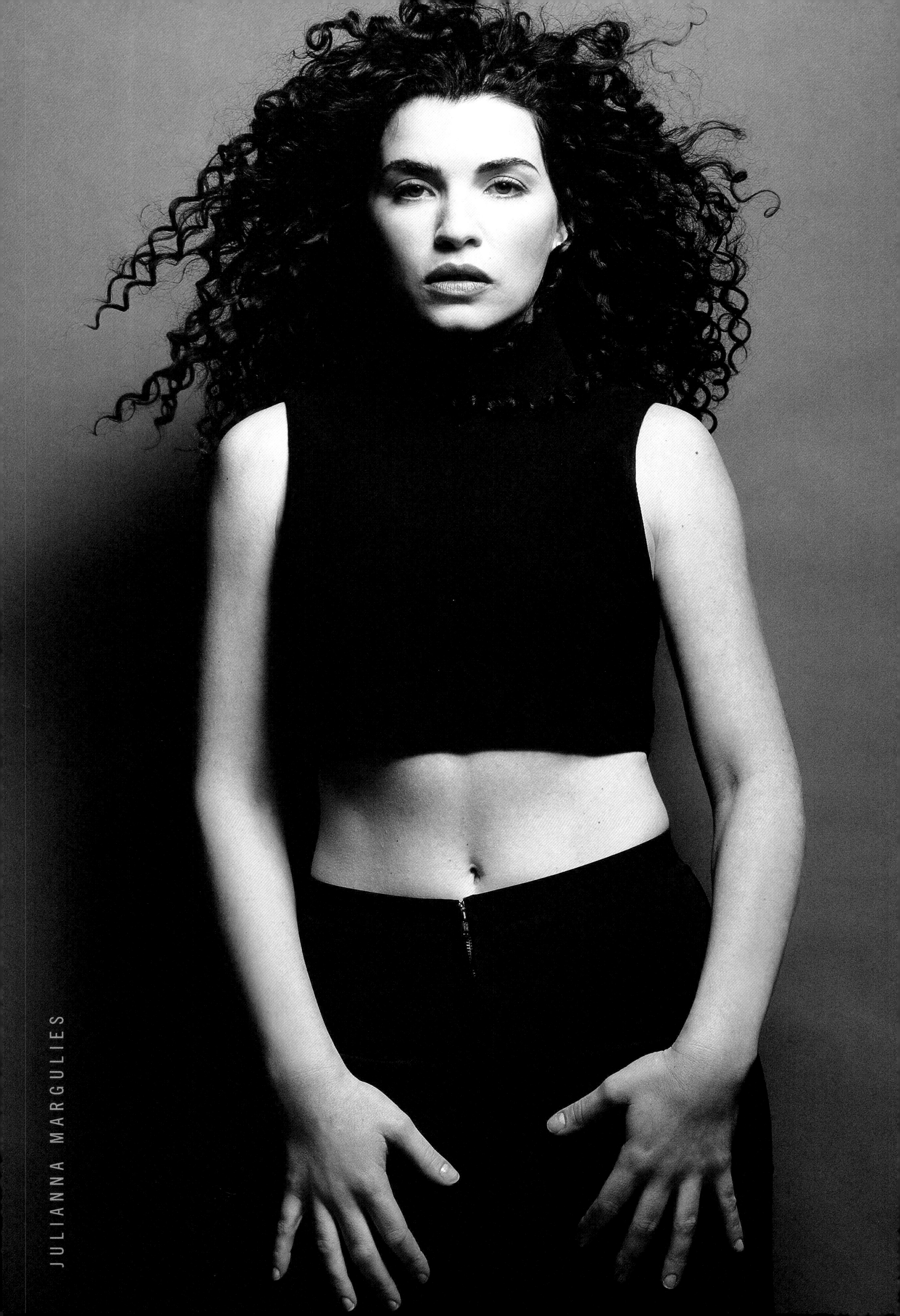

JULIANNA MARGULIES

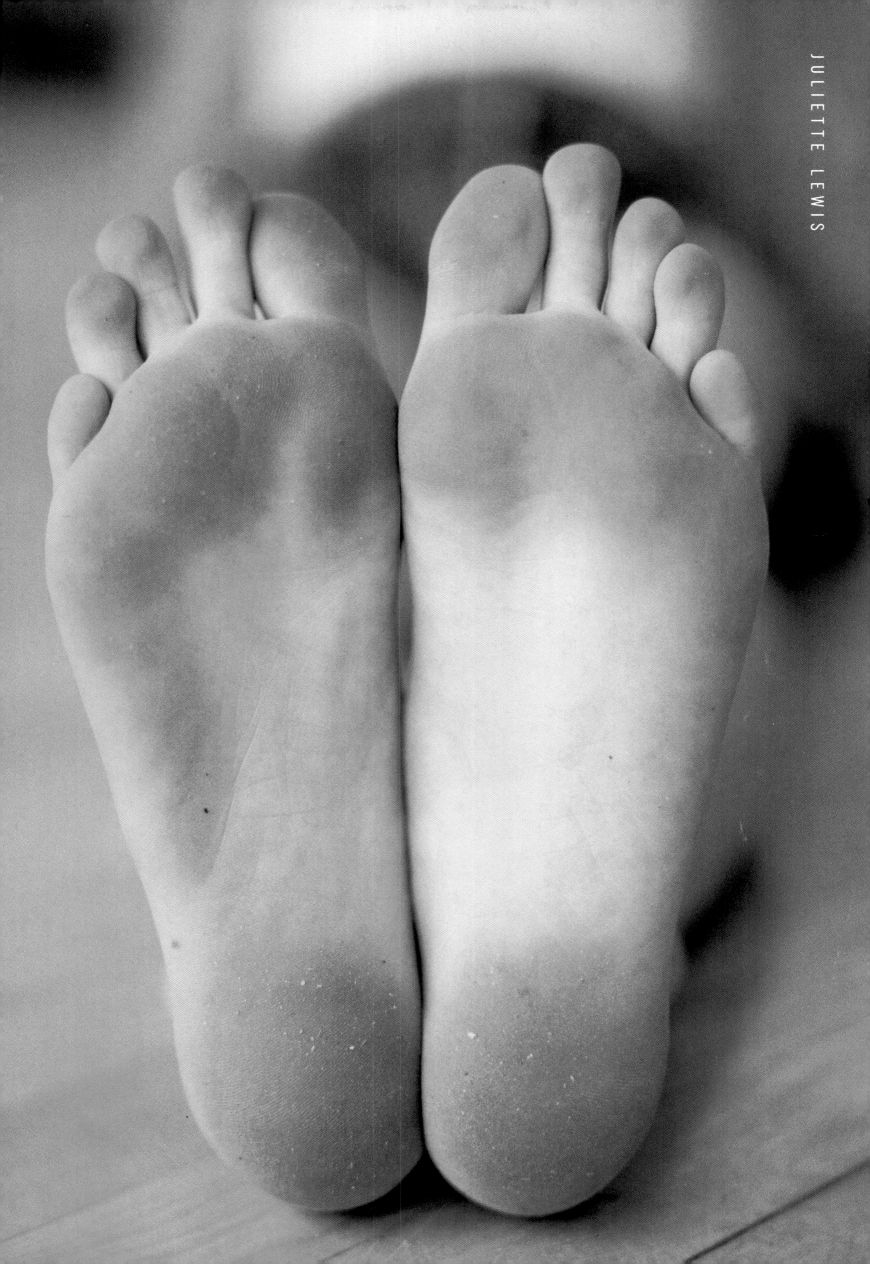

MY FIVE-YEAR-OLD son thinks everybody who vaguely resembles me is *me* – anyone blond with an angular face. So, he thinks Arnold Schwarzenegger is me, which is something I'm not going to tell him the truth about until he's about ten.

I THINK WHEN I was younger, I wanted to tell everybody every thing because I thought I was so damn interesting. Then I heard the snoring.

I HATE THAT FUCKIN' ROLE-MODEL SHIT. I am very flattered when people say I inspire them. I'm like: "Wow, that's deep. Thank you." But don't get mad at me if you see me in a club, humpin' on some fine-ass man's behind. Because I've got to live my life the way I see fit.

face of the planet. luckiest bitch on the ects, man. I'm the come from the projthen I think back: I And every now and name to his face. can call him by his the United States. I with the president of I GET TO HANG OUT

THE HARDEST PART about shooting a movie is getting up in the morning, just like any other job.

THE SINGLE WEIRDEST thing about being a celebrity, for lack of a better word, is that you meet other celebrities and they're strangers to you, but it doesn't seem like it. It feels like you already know them because you know so much about them.

I JUST HAVE TO TRUST that something I like, somthing that my staff likes and believes in, people will also like. If not then I'll be working at the Gap in a year. In the corduroy section, look for me.

say things that are funny. that are funny rather than I LIKE TO DO THINGS

GEORGE CLOONEY

JIM CARREY

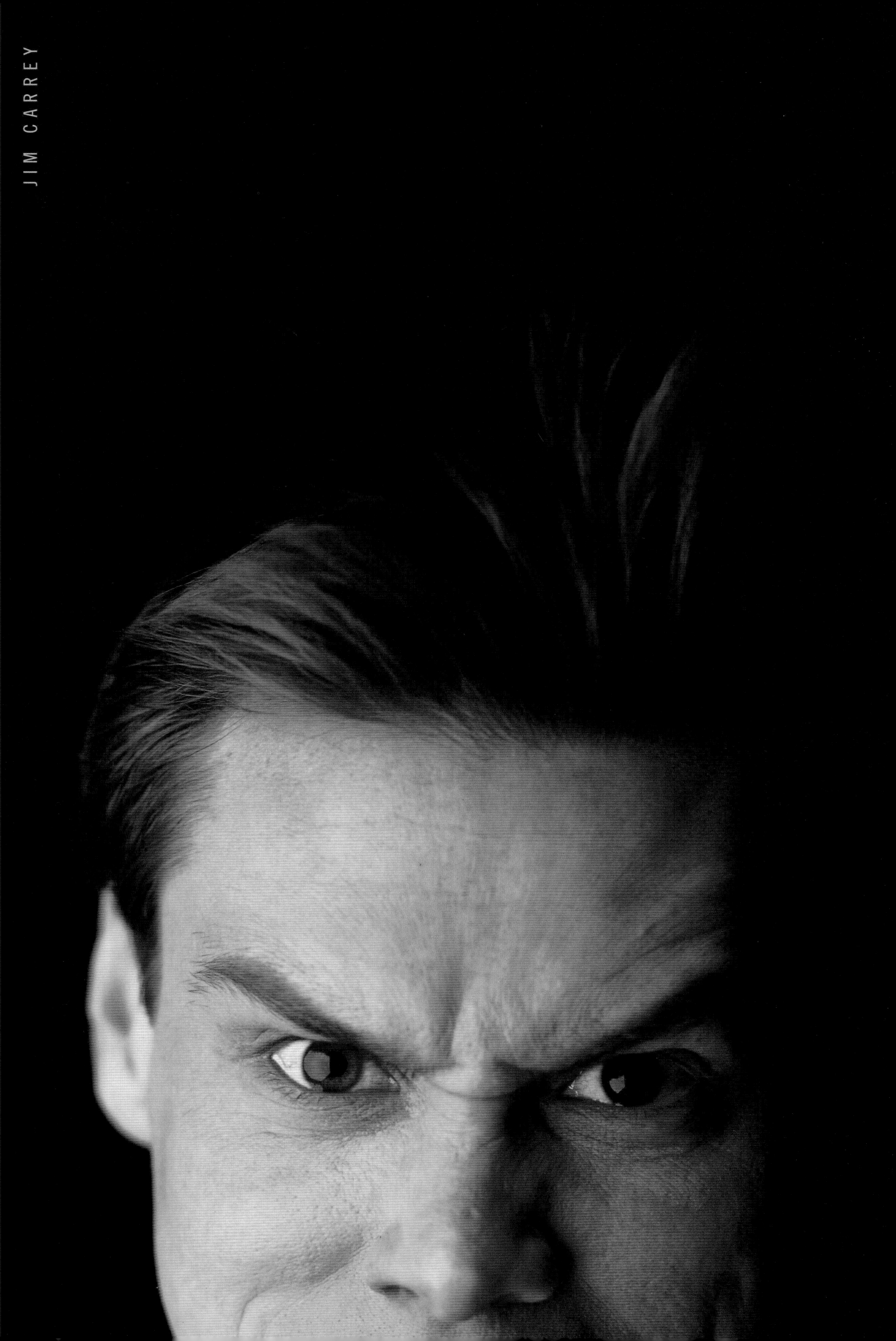

PHIL HARTMAN

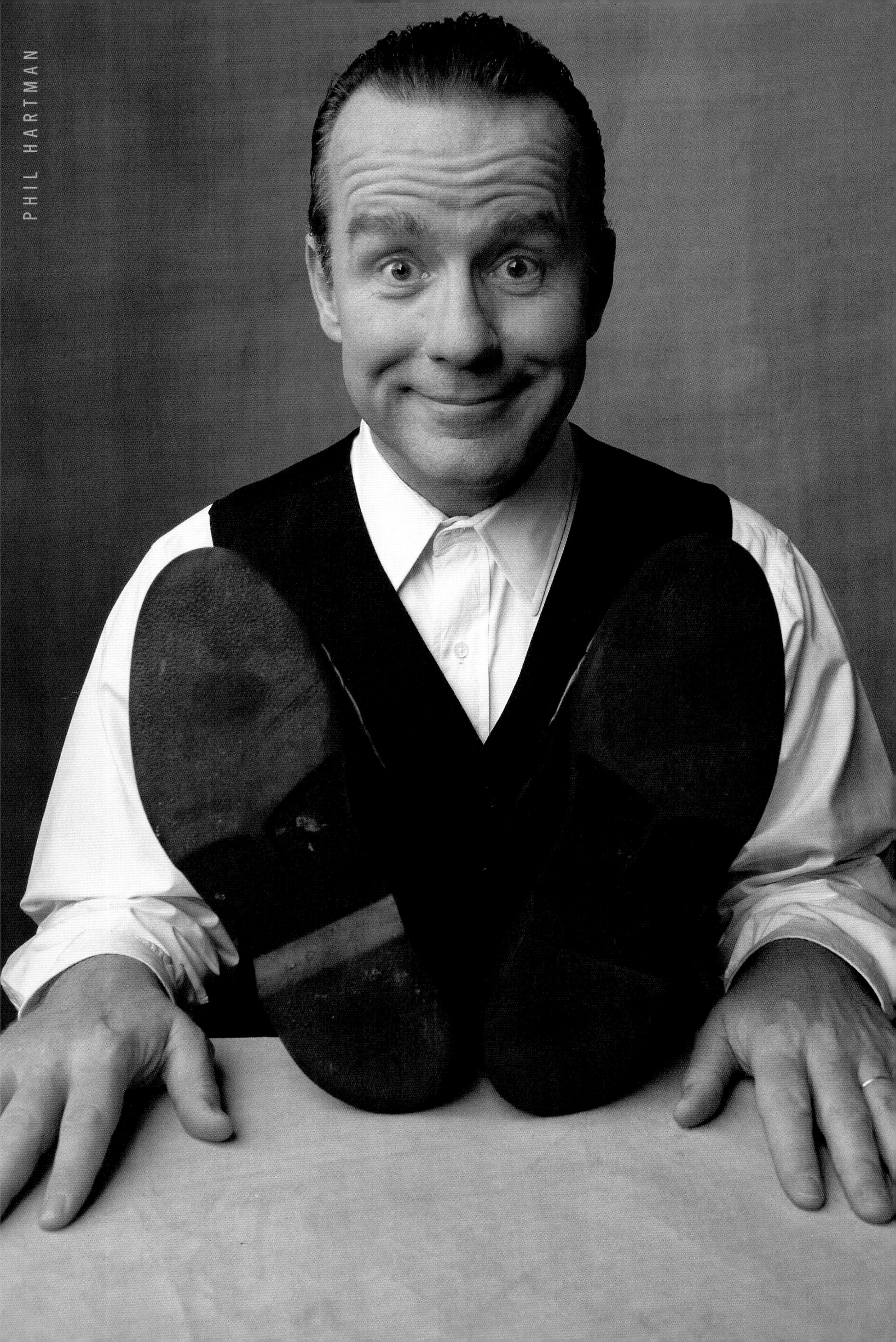

BRAD PITT	MARK SELIGER
ELISABETH SHUE	MARK SELIGER
PATRICK SWAYZE	MARY ELLEN MARK
COURTENEY COX	MARK SELIGER
DREW BARRYMORE	MARK SELIGER
JULIA LOUIS-DREYFUS & JERRY SEINFELD	MARK SELIGER
ANTONIO BANDERAS	LANCE STAEDLER
MELANIE GRIFFITH	NAOMI KALTMAN
KENNETH BRANAGH	ANDREW SOUTHAM
EMMA THOMPSON	NEIL DAVENPORT
PATRICIA ARQUETTE	BUTCH BELAIR
NICOLAS CAGE	DAVIS FACTOR
TOM CRUISE	LANCE STAEDLER
NICOLE KIDMAN	LANCE STAEDLER
KIM BASINGER & ALEC BALDWIN	LANCE STAEDLER
CHRISSIE HYNDE	MARK SELIGER
TYRA BANKS	KATE GARNER
HUGH GRANT	JON RAGEL
KATO KAELIN	MARY ELLEN MARK
TOM HANKS	MARK SELIGER
JODIE FOSTER	MARK SELIGER
MATT DILLON	LANCE STAEDLER
ASHLEY JUDD	MARK SELIGER
LUKE PERRY	GREG GORMAN
JASON PRIESTLEY	LANCE STAEDLER
MEL GIBSON	PEGGY SIROTA
JANET JACKSON	GEORGE HOLZ
WHOOPI GOLDBERG	MARK SELIGER
JOHNNY DEPP	WAYNE MASER
GEENA DAVIS	LANCE STAEDLER
CINDY CRAWFORD	DAVIS FACTOR
QUENTIN TARANTINO	MARK SELIGER
MICHELLE PFEIFFER	BRIGITTE LACOMBE
DENIS LEARY	BUTCH BELAIR
LEA THOMPSON	MARK SELIGER
HELEN HUNT	MARK SELIGER
AIDAN QUINN	DAVID BAILEY
ANDREW SHUE	MARK SELIGER
ELISABETH SHUE	MARK SELIGER
SHARON STONE	ANDREW MacPHERSON
ROB MORROW	MARK SELIGER
MATT LeBLANC	STEPHEN DANELIAN
TREAT WILLIAMS	MARY ELLEN MARK
JERRY SEINFELD	FRANK OCKENFELS 3
MICHAEL RICHARDS	STEPHEN DANELIAN
JULIA LOUIS-DREYFUS	JON RAGEL
GARRY SHANDLING	MARK SELIGER
MELISSA ETHERIDGE	MARK SELIGER
VANESSA WILLIAMS	NAOMI KALTMAN
DENNIS HOPPER	ANDREW SOUTHAM
TIM BURTON	THE DOUGLAS BROTHERS
SEAN PENN	WILLY RIZZO
KEVIN SPACEY	ANDREW SOUTHAM
LEONARDO DiCAPRIO	MARK SELIGER
LISA LOEB	KEVIN WESTENBERG
KENNEDY	MARK SELIGER
MICHAEL STIPE	ANTON CORBIJN
COOLIO	ALBERT WATSON
LENNY KRAVITZ	RUVEN AFANADOR
RICHARD GERE	LANCE STAEDLER
PATRICK SWAYZE	LANCE STAEDLER

DWIGHT YOAKAM	DANIELA FEDERICI
CLINT BLACK	CATANZARO & MAHDESSIAN
MARIO VAN PEEBLES	MARK SELIGER
CAMERON DIAZ	BUTCH BELAIR
ALICIA SILVERSTONE	PEGGY SIROTA
CHRISTIAN SLATER	MARK SELIGER
GWYNETH PALTROW	STEVEN SEBRING
STEPHEN DORFF	MARK SELIGER
SAMUEL L. JACKSON	MELODIE McDANIEL
MEL GIBSON	PEGGY SIROTA
JOHN BARROWMAN	LYNDA CHURILLA
TIMOTHY HUTTON	JOHN HUBA
GARY OLDMAN	PEGGY SIROTA
CARRIE FISHER	MARK SELIGER
BRENDAN FRASER	DEWEY NICKS
COURTNEY LOVE	MARK SELIGER
JAKOB DYLAN	LEN IRISH
LIV TYLER	MARK SELIGER
WINONA RYDER	WAYNE MASER
ANGELA BASSETT	DAVIS FACTOR
K.D. LANG	STEPHEN DANELIAN
SALMA HAYEK	RUVEN AFANADOR
CHRIS ISAAK	MICHAEL MILLER
CHAZZ PALMINTERI	BUTCH BELAIR
MIRA SORVINO	GUZMAN
ROSIE PEREZ	DEWEY NICKS
JACK NICHOLSON	PEGGY SIROTA
NATALIE MERCHANT	FRANK OCKENFELS 3
LIZ PHAIR	STEPHANIE PFRIENDER
TORI AMOS	GUZMAN
STING	MAX VADUKUL
BJÖRK	KATE GARNER
BILLY ZANE	GREG GORMAN
GILLIAN ANDERSON	ANDREW SOUTHAM
DAVID DUCHOVNY	JON RAGEL
MARK WAHLBERG	DEWEY NICKS
SIEGFRIED & ROY	MARK SELIGER
TOM JONES	MARK SELIGER
JOHN GOODMAN	GREG GORMAN
MADONNA	STEVEN MEISEL
ELLEN BARKIN	MATTHEW ROLSTON
CAMERON DIAZ	BUTCH BELAIR
SARAH JESSICA PARKER	DEWEY NICKS
KEANU REEVES	SANTE D'ORAZIO
CHARLIE SHEEN	BUTCH BELAIR
LAURENCE FISHBURNE	STEPHEN DANELIAN
JULIANNA MARGULIES	MARK SELIGER
TOM HANKS	MARK SELIGER
JULIETTE LEWIS	PEGGY SIROTA
CONAN O'BRIEN	LEN IRISH
LISA KUDROW	DAVIS FACTOR
GEORGE CLOONEY	MARK SELIGER
MATTHEW PERRY	ANDREW D. BERSTEIN
HENRY ROLLINS	PEGGY SIROTA
JULIANA HATFIELD	ANDREW SOUTHAM
JIM CARREY	STEPHEN DANELIAN
SANDRA BULLOCK	KATE GARNER
PHIL HARTMAN	MARK SELIGER
DAVID SCHWIMMER	MARK SELIGER
BRAD PITT	MARK SELIGER

BRAD PITT